# ŠEVČÍK

## OPUS 2 PART 1

### SCHOOL OF BOWING
### TECHNIQUE

### SCHULE DER
### BOGENTECHNIK

### ÉCOLE DU MÉCANISME
### DE L'ARCHET

FOR

# CELLO

ARR. FEUILLARD

BOSWORTH

| Poznámka. | Примѣчаніе. |
|---|---|

*Obsažená zde cvičení smyccová dělí se na dvě skupiny:*

*a) cvičení pro pravou ruku (rámě): sešit I a II.*

*b) cvičení pro ohbí ruky: seš. III - VI.*

*Každá skupina tvoří pro sebe samostatný a uzavřený celek; ale obě skupiny musí současně býti studovány, poněvadž výcvik ramene s výcvikem ohbí ruky rovnoměrně má pokračovati. Po čísle 5 I.sešitu přikročí tedy žák ihned k cvičením sešitu III., poněvadž mu každodenně několik smykových cvičení pro rámě i pro ohbí ruky střídavě jest probrati.*

Настоящія упражненія распадаются на двѣ группы:

а) Упражненія для правой руки: тетради I и II.

б) Упражненія для кисти: тетради III - VI.

Каждая группа упражненій составляетъ самостоятельное и законченное цѣлое; но обѣ группы требуютъ совмѣстнаго изученія, такъ какъ развитіе руки должно идти параллельно съ развитіемъ кисти. Поэтому ученикъ, дойдя до No 5го Iой тетради, долженъ приступить также къ упражненіямъ IIIей тетради, чтобы разучивать ежедневно по нѣскольку упражненій для правой руки и кисти.

| *Zkratky a znamení:* | Сокращенія и знаки: |
|---|---|

| | *Czech* | *Russian* |
|---|---|---|
| G. | *celým smyccem.* | Цѣлымъ смычкомъ. |
| H. | *polovičním smyccem.* | Половиною смычка. |
| u.H. | *dolejší polovicí.* | Нижнею половиною. |
| o.H. | *hořejší polovicí.* | Верхнею половиною. |
| ⅓ B. | *třetinou smyčce.* | Одною третью смычка. |
| Fr. | *U žabky smyčce.* | У колодочки. |
| M. | *Ve středu smyčce* | Серединою смычка. |
| Sp. | *U hrotu smyčce.* | Концомъ смычка. |
| M* | *Středem, pak u hrotu a u žabky.* | Серединою, затѣмъ концомъ и у колодочки. |
| Π | *Smyk dolů.*) | Смычкомъ внизъ.*) |
| V | *Smyk nahoru.* | Смычкомъ вверхъ |
| — | *široký smyk.**)* | Протяжнымъ штрихомъ.**) |
| • | *trhaně nebo úderem.* | Отрывисто. |
| ᛉ | *tepem (spiccato) aneb skákavě.* | Отскакивающимъ или прыгающимъ смычкомъ. |
| ) | *zdvih smyčce.* | Снять смычокъ. |

---

*) Když na počátku cvičení žádné znaménko udano. není, bere se první tón vždy u žabky a Π.

**) Noty, u nichž není smyk-poznamenán, hrají se vyrážene.

*) Если въ началѣ упражненія нѣтъ никакого знака, то нужно начинать всегда первую ноту у колодочки внизъ.

**) Ноты, не обозначенныя никакимъ штрихомъ, играются попеременно внизъ-вверхъ.

| Anmerkung. | Remarque. | Note. |
|---|---|---|

Die vorliegenden Bogenübungen zerfallen in zwei Gruppen:

a) Uebungen für den rechten Arm: Heft I und II.

b) Uebungen für das Handgelenk: Heft III - VI.

Jede Gruppe bildet ein selbständiges und abgeschlossenes Ganze; doch erfordern beide Gruppen ein gleichzeitiges Studium, indem die Ausbildung des Armes parallel mit der Ausbildung des Handgelenkes vorschreiten soll. Bei № 5 des I^{ten} Heftes angelangt, schreitet darum der Schüler auch zu den Uebungen des III^{ten} Heftes, um täglich einige Bogenstrichübungen sowohl für den Arm, als auch für das Handgelenk vorzunehmen.

Ces exercices se divisent en deux groupes:

a) Exercices pour le bras droit, cahier I et II.

b) Exercices pour le poignet, cahier III - VI.

Chaque groupe d'exercices forme une partie indépendante et séparée; pourtant les deux groupes doivent être étudiés en même temps afin que le développement du bras droit s'avance parallèlement avec le développement du poignet. C'est pour cette raison que l'élève, arrivé au № 5 du I^{er} cahier, doit s'occuper aussi des exercices du III^{me} cahier, en travaillant chaque jour quelques coups d'archet pour le bras et pour le poignet.

The bowing-exercises presented here are divided into two groups:

a) Exercises for the Right Arm. Parts I and II.

b) Exercises for the Wrist. Parts III to VI.

Each group is independent and complete in itself, but the two groups must be studied simultaneously, because the training of the arm must proceed parallel with that of the wrist. When the student has reached № 5 of Part I, it is necessary for him to, at the same time, occupy himself with the exercises contained in Part III, in order to have for daily practice a few bowing-exercises for both the arm and the wrist.

| Abkürzungen und Zeichen: | Abréviations et signes: | Abbreviations and Signs: |
|---|---|---|

| | Abkürzungen und Zeichen | Abréviations et signes | Abbreviations and Signs |
|---|---|---|---|
| G. | Ganzer Bogen. | Tout l'archet. | Whole length of bow. |
| H. | Halber Bogen. | Moitié de l'archet. | Half length of bow. |
| u.H. | Untere Hälfte. | La moitié inférieure. | Lower half of bow. |
| o.H. | Obere Hälfte. | La moitié supérieure. | Upper half of bow. |
| ⅓ B. | Ein Drittel des Bogens. | Un tiers de l'archet. | ⅓^{rd} of bow-length. |
| Fr. | Am Frosch des Bogens. | Talon de l'archet. | Frog-end of bow. |
| M. | Mitte des Bogens. | Milieu de l'archet. | Middle of bow. |
| Sp. | Spitze des Bogens. | Pointe de l'archet. | Tip-end of bow. |
| M* | In der Mitte, dann an der Spitze und am Frosch. | Du milieu, puis de la pointe et du talon. | In the middle, and then at the tip and at the frog. |
| ⊓ | Herunterstrich.*) | Tirez.*) | Down-stroke.*) |
| V | Hinaufstrich. | Poussez. | Up-stroke. |
| – | Breit stossen.**) | Détaché large.**) | Broadly detached.**) |
| · | Abgestossen oder gehämmert. | Staccato ou martelé. | Staccato (chopped), or martellato (hammered). |
| ' | Geworfen (spiccato) oder springend (sautillé). | Jeté (spiccato) ou sautillé. | Spiccato (thrown), or saltato (sautillé, or hopping). |
| ) | Bogen heben. | Lever l'archet. | Raise the bow from the string. |

Aus Op.2 Heft 1-6 erschienen die Uebungsthemen in einem separaten Heft, um die Anschaffung von zwei Exemplaren zu ersparen.

*) Wenn am Anfange einer Uebung kein Zeichen beigesetzt ist, so fängt die erste Note immer am Frosch im Herunterstrich an.

**) Noten, über welchen kein Bogenstrich gesetzt ist, werden gestossen gespielt.

*) S'il n'y a pas de signe au commencement d'un exercice, on commence toujours la première note du talon en tirant.

**) Il faut détacher toutes les notes, dont le coup d'archet n'est pas marqué.

*) If no sign is shown at the beginning of an exercise, always begin the first note at the frog, with the down-stroke.

**) Where no style of stroke is specified, each note is to be detached.

ERSTE ABTEILUNG (Heft I). Vorübungen. | PREMIERE PARTIE (Cahier I). Exercices préparatoires. PRVNÍ DÍL (Sešil I). Průprava. | PART I (Section I). Preparatory exercises. ПЕРВАЯ ЧАСТЬ (Тетрадь I). Начальныя упражненія.

Edited and translated by H. Brett.
Edited by L. R. Feuillard and A. E. Bosworth.

## № 1.

**Haltung des Bogens.**
Man übe das folgende Beispiel mit ganz wenig Bogen a) in der Mitte, b) an der Spitze, c) am Frosch. Während der Pausen den Bogen auf der Saite liegen lassen und laut den Takt zählen.

**Tenue de l'archet.**
On travaillera l'exemple suivant avec très peu d'archet a) du milieu, b) de la pointe, c) du talon. Pendant les silences laisser l'archet à la corde et compter à haute voix.

*Držení smyčce.*
*Následovní cvičení cvič jen malou částí smyčce a) uprostřed, b) y hrotu, c) u žabky. Při pomlkách nech smyčec spočívat na struně a počítej nahlas takt.*

**How to hold the bow.**
Practice the following example with very little bow-length: a) in the middle; b) at the tip; c) at the heel. During the pauses allow the bow to rest on the string and count the beats of the bar out loud.

**Держаніе смычка.**
Слѣдующій примѣръ исполнять возможно короткимъ штрихомъ а) на серединѣ, б) на концѣ, в) у колодочки. Во время паузъ смычка не снимать и считать вслухъ.

Beispiel. Exemple. Příklad. Example. Примѣръ.

## № 2.

**Führung des Bogens.**
Die untenstehenden 18 Beispiele sind auf folgende VI Arten auszuführen.

**Mouvement de l'archet.**
Exécutez les 18 exemples ci-dessous des VI manières suivantes:

*Pohyby smyčce.*
*Dole uvedených 18 příkladů prober na šesterý způsob.*

**Movements of the bow.**
Play the 18 examples below without raising the bow, in the following VI styles:

**Движенія смычка.**
Приведенные ниже 18 примѣровъ исполнять слѣдующими шестью способами:

Mit ganzem Bogen. / Tout l'archet. / Celým smyčcem. / Whole bow. / Цѣлымъ смычкомъ.

Mit halbem Bogen. / Moitié de l'archet. / Polovicí smyčce. / Half length. / Половиною смычка.

Mit der Mitte des Bogens. / Du milieu de l'archet. / Středem smyčce. / Bow-middle. / Серединою смычка.

Beispiele. Exemples. Příklady. Examples. Примѣры.

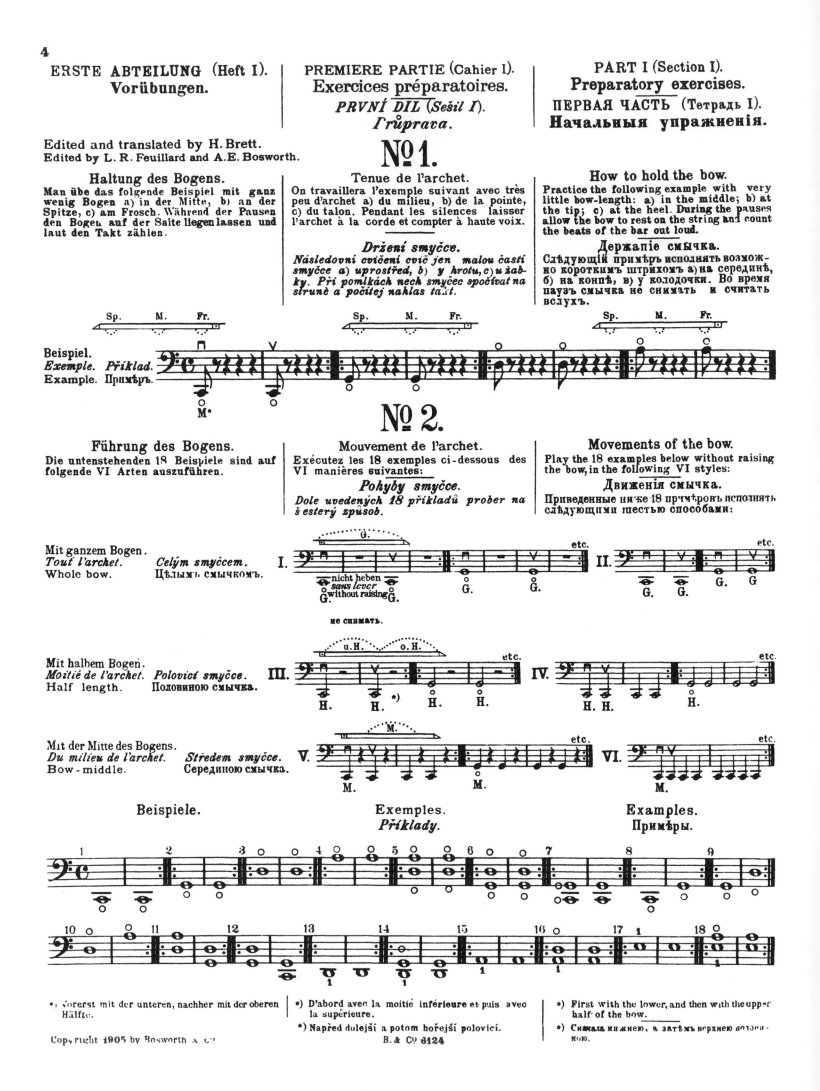

*) Vorerst mit der unteren, nachher mit der oberen Hälfte.

*) D'abord avec la moitié inférieure et puis avec la supérieure.
*) Napřed dolejší a potom hořejší polovicí.

*) First with the lower, and then with the upper half of the bow.
*) Сначала нижнею, а затѣмъ верхнею половиною.

Copyright 1905 by Bosworth & Co.

B. & Cº 8124

# Rhythmische Uebungen und Einteilung des Bogens. | Exercices rhythmiques et division de l'archet. | Rhythmic exercises and dividing of the bow-length.

*Rhytmická cvičení a rozdělení smyčce.* | Ритмическія упражненія и дѣленіе смычка.

## №·3.

Beispiel in ganzen Noten mit 57 Varianten.
Jede Variante ist auf dem ganzen Beispiele durchzuführen. | Exemple en rondes avec 57 variantes. Il faut travailler chaque variante sur tout l'exemple. | Example in semibreves (whole notes) with 57 variations. Practice each variation right through the whole of each example.

*Příklady o celých notách s 57 změnami.*
*Každá změna nechť se probere na celém příkladu.* | Примѣръ цѣлыми нотами съ 57 варіантами. Каждый варіантъ играть на цѣломъ примѣрѣ.

Varianten des vorhergehenden Beispieles. | Variantes sur l'exemple précédent. | Variations on the preceding example.
*Obměny předcházejícího příkladu.* | Варіанты предыдущаго примѣра.

B. & Cᵒ 6124

6

# № 4.

Etude in halben Noten mit 75 Varianten in der ersten Lage.

Etude en blanches avec 75 variantes à la 1ère Position.

*Cvičení v půlových notách s 75 variantami v první poloze.*

Study in minims (half-notes) with 75 variations in the First Position.

Этюдъ полунотами съ 75 варіантами въ первой позиціи.

Varianten.  |  Variantes. *Změny.*  |  Variations. Варіанты.

Mit ganzem Bogen.
*Tout l'archet.*
Whole bow-length.

*Celým smyccem.*
Цѣлымъ смычкомъ.

Mit halbem Bogen.
*Moitié de l'archet.*
Half bow-length.

*Polovicí smyčce.*
Половиною смычка.

Mit der unteren, dann mit der oberen Hälfte.
*Avec la moitié inférieure, puis avec la supérieure.*
First with lower, then with upper half length.

*Napřed dolejší a pak hořejší polovicí smyčce.*
Нижнею, затѣмъ верхнею половиною.

*) Varianten 9-14 mit derselben Metronombezeichnung.

*) Les variantes 9-14 du même mouvement du métronome.

*) Variations 9 to 14 with the same metronomic rhythm.

*) Změny 9-14 s týmže metronomickým označením.

*) Варіанты 9-14 тѣмъ-же движеніемъ метронома.

B. & Cᵒ 6124

## Stricharten mit liegendem und springendem Bogen.

## Coups d'archet détachés et rebondissants.

*Druhy smyků ležícím a skákavým smyčcem.*

## Detached and hopping styles of bowing.

Движенія лежащимъ и отскакивающимъ смычкомъ.

# № 5. *)

**Etude in Vierteln mit 260 Varianten.**
Um die Bogenführung auf hohen Lagen auszubilden, sollen die Varianten auch in den Daumenlagen geübt werden. Siehe № 8.

**Etude en noires avec 260 variantes.**
Pour développer l'archet dans les positions élevées il faut étudier aussi les variantes aux positions du pouce. Voir № 8.

**Study in crotchets with 260 Variations.**
In order to develop the bowing in the high positions, the Variations must be practiced in the Positions of the Thumb as well. See № 8.

*Cvičení ve čtvrtích o 260 změnách.*
*Aby vedení smyčce také ve vysokých polohách bylo dokonalé, musí tyto varianty cvičiti se také v poloze palcové. Viz str. 8.*

Этюдъ четвертными съ 260 варіантами. Для развитія движеній смычка на высокихъ позиціяхъ, варіанты должны быть исполняемы также въ позиціяхъ большого пальца. См. стр. 8.

*) Siehe Anmerkung, Seite 2 und 3.     *) Voir la remarque de la page 2 et 3.     *) See note, page 2 and 3.

*) Viz poznámku na str. 2 a 3.     *) См. примѣчаніе стр 2 и 3.

B. & Cᵒ 6124

Staccato mit dem Handgelenk.*)
*Staccato du poignet.*\*)
Staccato from the wrist.*)

*Staccato obhím ruky.*\*)
Стаккато кистью.*)

*) Gleichzeitig mit den Stricharten 136-260 sind auch die Stricharten 1-109 aus № 6 vorzunehmen.

*) En même temps que l'étude des coups d'archet 136-260 on travaillera aussi les coups d'archet 1-109 du № 6.

*) Simultaneously with the bowing-styles 136 to 260, the bowing-styles 1 to 109 of № 6 must be practiced.

*) Zároveň s druhy smyku 136-260 jest cvičiti i druhy smyku 1-109 z čís. 6.

*) Одновременно съ движеніями смычка 136-260 слѣдуетъ проходить также движенія смычка 1-109 изъ № 6.

B. & C⁰ 6124

*) Zeichen ) zeigt an, wann der Bogen gehoben werden soll.

*) Le signe ) indique, qu'il faut lever l'archet.

*) Značka ) ukazuje, kdy se má smyčec zdvihnouti.

*) The sign ) shows where the bow must be raised.

*) Знакъ ) показываетъ, когда нужно снять смычокъ въ первый разъ.

Fliegendes Staccato.
*Staccato volant.*
Flying staccato.

*Létavé staccato.*
Летучее стаккато.

Geworfenes Staccato.
*Staccato jeté.*
Thrown staccato.

*Staccato úhozem.*
Отскакивающее ст.

Im Herunterstrich am Frosch.
*En tirant du talon.*
Down-stroke at the frog.

*Smykem u žabky dolů.*
Нижнимъ концомъ внизъ.

Im Hinaufstrich am Frosch.
*En poussant du talon.*
Up-stroke at the frog.

*Od žabky nahoru.*
Нижнимъ концомъ вверхъ.

Mit der Spitze im Hinaufstrich anschlagen.(Ṽ)
*Frappez de la pointe en poussant.(Ṽ)*
Up-stroke at the tip, as if striking.(Ṽ)

*Úhoz hrotem při smyku nahoru.*
Ударить концомъ смычка, вверхъ. (Ṽ)

*Crescendo-
decrescendo.*

B. & Cᵒ 6124

# № 6.

Etude in Achteln mit 214 Veränderungen des Bogenstriches.

Dieselbe in der Daumenlage, siehe № 10.

Etude en croches avec 214 changements de coups d'archet.

*Cvičení v osminách s 214 změnami smyku.*

La même à la position du pouce, voir № 10.

*Totéž v poloze palcové Viz čís. 10.*

Study in quavers (eighth-notes) with 214 changes of bowing-styles.

The like in the Position of the Thumb, see № 10.

Тотъ-же этюдъ въ позиціи большого пальца. См.№ 10.

**Allegro moderato.**

Б. & Cº 6124

18

# №7.

Etude in Achteln (6/8 Takt) mit 91 Veränderungen des Bogenstriches.

Dieselbe in der Daumenlage, siehe № 9.

Etude en croches (mesure 6/8) avec 91 changements de coups d'archet.

*Cvičení v osminách (6/8 takt) s 91 proměnami smyku.*

La même à la position du pouce, voir №9.

*Totéž v poloze palcové, viz čís. 9.*

Study in quavers (eighth-notes) in 6/8 time, with 91 changes of bowing-styles.

Этюдъ восьмыми (въ 6/8 тактѣ) съ 91 перемѣнами движенія смычка.

The same in the Position of the Thumb, see №9.

Тотъ-же этюдъ въ позиціи большого пальца. См. № 9.

B. & Cᵒ 6124

Mit dem Handgelenk. (Métr: ♩.=76)
*Du poignet.*
From the wrist.

*Ohbím ruky.*
Кистью.

Punktierte Sechzehntel.
*Doubles croches pointées.*
Dotted semiquavers (sixteenth-notes). (Métr: ♩.=60)

*Tečkované šestnáctiny.*
Шестнадцатыя съ точкою.

(Métr: ♪=168)
*Spiccato.*

(Métr: ♪=160)
*Sautillé.*

(Métr: ♩.=66)

B. & Cⁱᵉ 6124

Anwendung der vorhergehenden Bogenübungen in den Daumenlagen.

Emploi des exercices d'archet précédents aux positions du pouce.

*Provedení předešlých cvičení v poloze palcové.*

Employment of the foregoing bowing-exercises in the Positions of the Thumb.

Примѣненіе предыдущихъ смычковыхъ упражненій въ позиціяхъ большого пальца.

## № 8.

Mit Stricharten aus № 5.

Avec les coups d'archet du № 5.
*Smyky z čís. 5.*

With the bowings of № 5.
Движеніями смычка изъ № 5.

Daumenlage.*)
*Position du pouce.*)
Position of the Thumb.*)

*Poloha palcová.*)
Позиція большого пальца.*)

## № 9.

Mit Stricharten aus № 7.

Avec les coups d'archet du № 7.
*Smyky z čís. 7.*

With the bowings of № 7.
Движеніями смычка изъ № 7.

Daumenlage.*)
*Position du pouce.*)
Position of the Thumb.*)

*Poloha palcová.*)
Позиція большого пальца.*)

## № 10.

Mit Stricharten aus № 6.

Avec les coups d'archet du № 6.
*Smyky z čís. 6.*

With the bowings of № 6.
Движеніями смычка изъ № 6.

Daumenlage.*)
*Position du pouce.*)
Position of the Thumb.*)

*Poloha palcová.*)
Позиція большого пальца.*)

*) Der Daumen darf während der ganzen Übung seinen Platz nicht verändern.

*) Le pouce ne doit pas changer de place pendant tout l'exercice.
*) Poloha palce nesmí se během tohoto cvičení změniti.

*) The thumb must not change its place during the whole exercise.
*) Большой палецъ не долженъ мѣнять свое положеніе въ теченіе цѣлаго упражненія.

Uebungen in gebrochenen Akkorden auf 3 und 4 Saiten mit Anwendung der vorhergehenden Bogenstrichübungen.

Exercices en accords brisés sur 3 et 4 cordes en appliquant les exercices d'archet précédents.

*Cvičení v lomených akkordech na 3 a 4 strunách podlé předešlých cvičení smykových.*

Exercises in arpeggios (broken chords) on 3 and 4 strings, using the preceding bowing-exercises.

Упражненія ломанными аккордами на 3 и 4 струнахъ съ примѣненіемъ предыдущихъ упражненій для смычка.

## № 11.

Mit Stricharten 1-198 aus № 6.

Avec les coups d'archet 1-198 du №6.
*Smyky 1-198 z čís. 6.*

With the bowings 1 to 198 of №6.
Движеніями смычка 1-198 изъ № 6.

## № 12.

Mit Stricharten 1-198 aus № 6.

Avec les coups d'archet 1-198 du №6.
*Smyky 1-198 z čís. 6.*

With the bowings 1 to 198 of №6.
Движеніями смычка 1-198 изъ № 6.

Daumenlage.*)
*Position du pouce.*)*
Position of the Thumb.*)

*Poloha palcová.*)*
Позиція большого пальца.*)

*) Der Daumen darf während der ganzen Übung seinen Platz nicht verändern.

*) Le pouce ne doit pas changer de place pendant tout l'exercice.

*) Palec po celé cvičení nezmění svou polohu.

*) The thumb must not change its place during the whole exercise.

*) Большой палецъ не долженъ мѣнять свое положеніе въ теченіе цѣлаго упражненія.

B. & Cᵒ 6424